DINO DUEL

GIGANOTOSAURUS VS. ARGENTINOSAURUS

Prehistoric Showdown

Tom Jackson

Lerner Publications ◆ Minneapolis

Lerner Publications Company
An imprint of Lerner Publishing Group, Inc.
241 First Avenue North
Minneapolis, MN 55401 USA

For reading levels and more information, look up this title at www.lernerbooks.com.

Main body text set in Aptifer Sans LT Pro.
Typeface provided by Linotype.

Library of Congress Cataloging-in-Publication Data

Names: Jackson, Tom, 1972–author
Title: Giganotosaurus vs. argentinosaurus : prehistoric showdown / Tom Jackson.
Other titles: Giganotosaurus versus argentinosaurus
Description: Minneapolis : Lerner Publications, [2026] | Series: Dino duel | Includes bibliographical references and index. | Audience term: juvenile | Audience: Ages 8–11 Lerner Publications | Audience: Grades 4–6 Lerner Publications | Summary: “Argentinosaurus might be larger than giganotosaurus, but with its strong bite and speed, giganotosaurus can still prey on the larger dinosaur. Discover these dinosaurs’ strengths and weaknesses, and who might win in the fight for survival”—Provided by publisher.
Identifiers: LCCN 2024043990 (print) | LCCN 2024043991 (ebook) | ISBN 9798765669235 lib. bdg. | ISBN 9798765683903 pbk | ISBN 9798765676653 epub
Subjects: LCSH: Giganotosaurus—Juvenile literature | Argentinosaurus—Juvenile literature
Classification: LCC QE862.S3 J3285 2026 (print) | LCC QE862.S3 (ebook) | DDC 567.912—dc23/eng/20250215

LC record available at https://lccn.loc.gov/2024043990
LC ebook record available at https://lccn.loc.gov/2024043991

Manufactured in the United States of America
1 – CG – 7/15/25

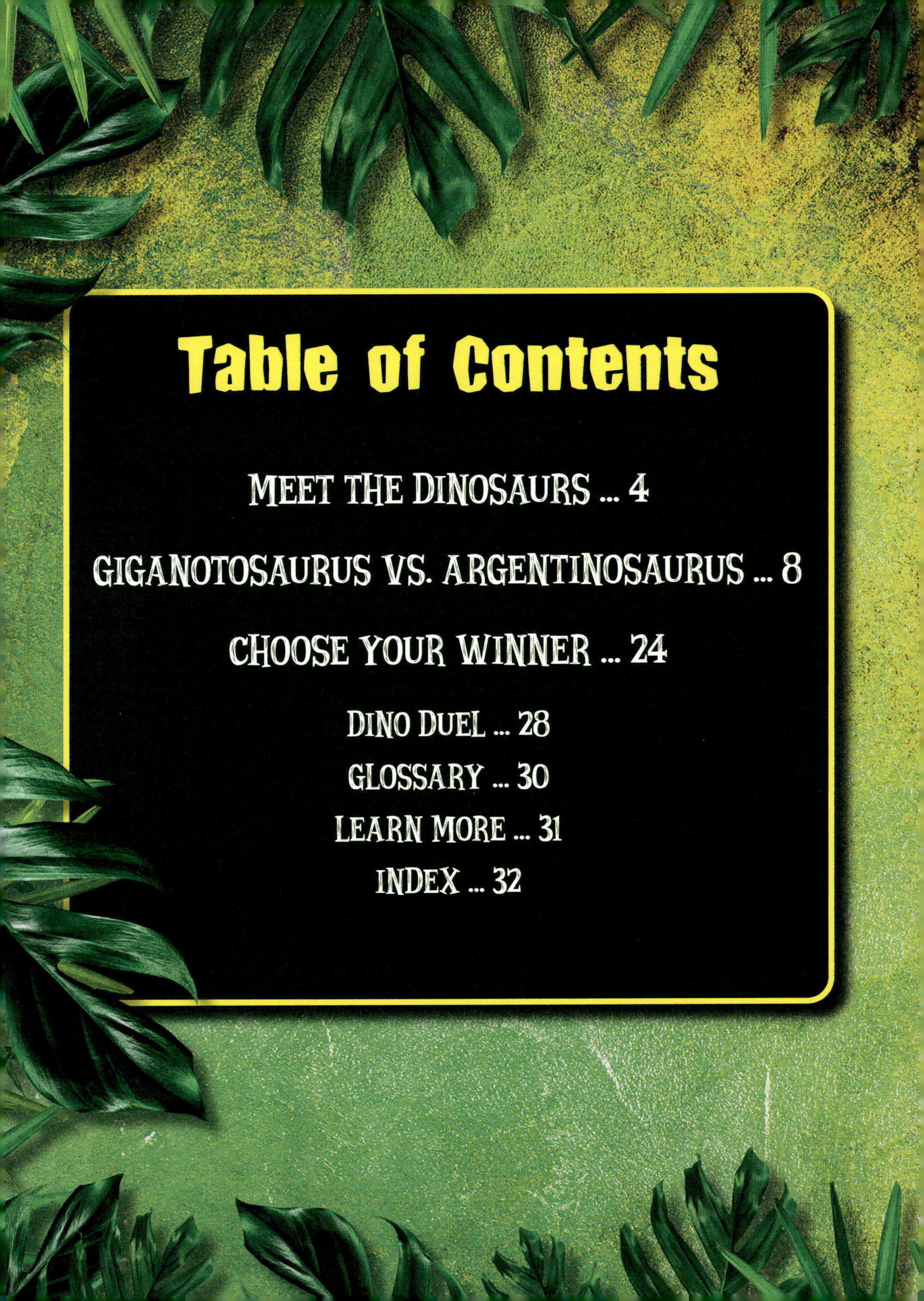

Table of Contents

MEET THE DINOSAURS

It has just stopped raining, and the forest is hot and steamy. A giganotosaurus is hungry. It lives in a small group, or pack. The pack has found the body of a dead dinosaur. They are ripping off small scraps of meat. There is not much to eat, so the giganotosaurus goes off alone looking for more food.

The big meat-eating dinosaur walks quietly through the trees. Then it sees something. Along the edge of the woodland is a herd of giant Argentinosauruses. They have very long necks. They can reach right up to the tops of the tallest trees. Up there, they can eat the leaves.

The giant dinosaurs stop eating and start to move away from the trees. They are heading out to an open area. They have been frightened by something. Maybe they can smell or hear the giganotosaurus. The leaf-eating dinosaurs are coming together to form a herd. Now the giganotosaurus can see that there are baby Argentinosauruses in their group.

Both these dinosaurs were some of the largest around at the time.

DINO STATS

Giganotosaurus

Weight: 7.2 tons (6.5 t)
Length: 41 feet (12.5 m)
Main weapons: Powerful bite, speed, strength

Argentinosaurus

Weight: 99 tons (90 t)
Length: 98 feet (30 m)
Main weapons: Long neck, large size and weight

The giganotosaurus is so hungry that it decides to attack. It will use its speed to rush in, then it will use its powerful bite. It will aim for a smaller Argentinosaurus. The adult Argentinosauruses will fight to protect them. They are ten times bigger than the giganotosaurus. Who will win this fight?

GIGANOTOSAURUS VS. ARGENTINOSAURUS

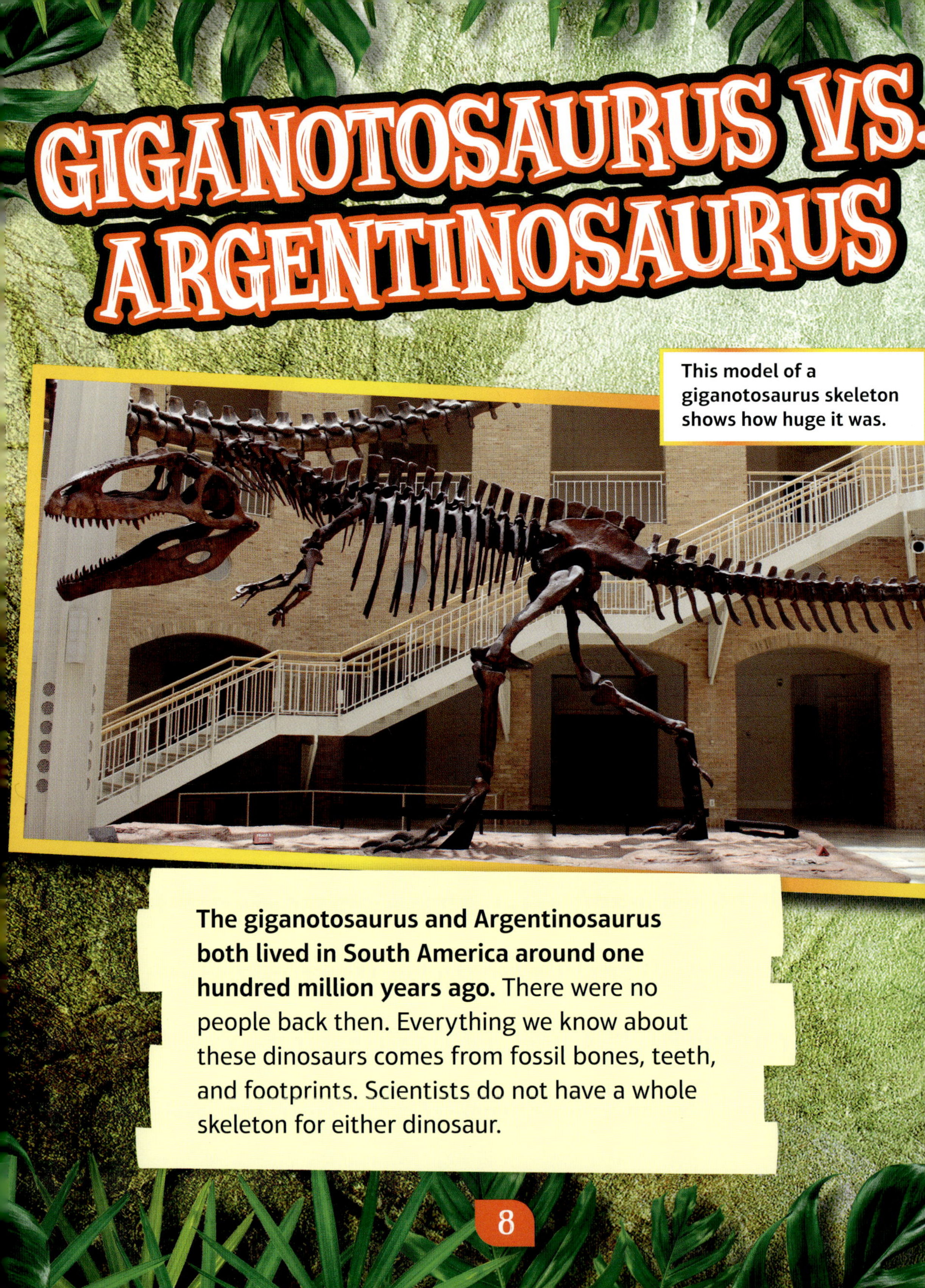

This model of a giganotosaurus skeleton shows how huge it was.

The giganotosaurus and Argentinosaurus both lived in South America around one hundred million years ago. There were no people back then. Everything we know about these dinosaurs comes from fossil bones, teeth, and footprints. Scientists do not have a whole skeleton for either dinosaur.

This is just one of several giant bones that made up an Argentinosaurus's spine.

The fossil teeth of a giganotosaurus tell us that they ate meat. Their teeth, claws, and leg bones were huge, and they show scientists how a giganotosaurus moved and killed its prey. They think giganotosauruses were one of the largest hunting dinosaurs. Argentinosaurus fossils show they were much bigger. They were nearly 100 feet (30 m) long!

Giant Animals

Both the Argentinosaurus and giganotosaurus were very large dinosaurs. The Argentinosaurus may be the largest dinosaur that ever lived. Fossil scientists have looked at the thickness of their bones. They say that Argentinosauruses could not grow much bigger or heavier. If they did, their bones would crack under the weight.

An Argentinosaurus's thigh bone was 8.2 feet (2.5 m) long. That's even taller than a pro basketball player! Each of the bones in its back was the size of a washing machine!

The giganotosaurus was a relative of the T. rex, another dinosaur predator. Giganotosauruses were even bigger than the T. rex! They were around 13 feet (4 m) tall. Their skull was nearly 6 feet (1.8 m) long. Giganotosauruses also had a long, flexible tail compared to other hunting dinosaurs. However, it was still only half as long as an Argentinosaurus's tail.

Checking Speed

A giganotosaurus walked and ran on two legs. An Argentinosaurus always moved on four legs. There was a big difference in the top speeds of the two dinosaurs. An Argentinosaurus's heavy legs had thick, cushioned sections called cartilage. These stopped the bones from being damaged as the dinosaur walked. It could not run at all. Scientists have calculated that an Argentinosaurus moved at a top speed of 5 miles (8 km) per hour.

Giganotosauruses were much faster. They rarely stood upright. Instead they leaned forward so their big head was balanced by their long tail. This meant the dinosaur could charge along on its powerful back legs. A giganotosaurus might have run around 30 miles (48 km) per hour. That's about as fast as a car!

Some scientists disagree that large two-legged dinosaurs like giganotosauruses could run fast. They think that the animal's long legs could only move fast enough for walking.

Eggs and Nests

Both Argentinosauruses and giganotosauruses laid eggs. No fossils of giganotosaurus eggs have been found yet. It is likely that they built a nest for them. Two-legged dinosaurs like the giganotosaurus were called therapods. We know more about other therapod dinosaurs. Many of them dug holes for their eggs and covered them in dirt and leaves to keep them warm. It is possible that giganotosauruses did this too.

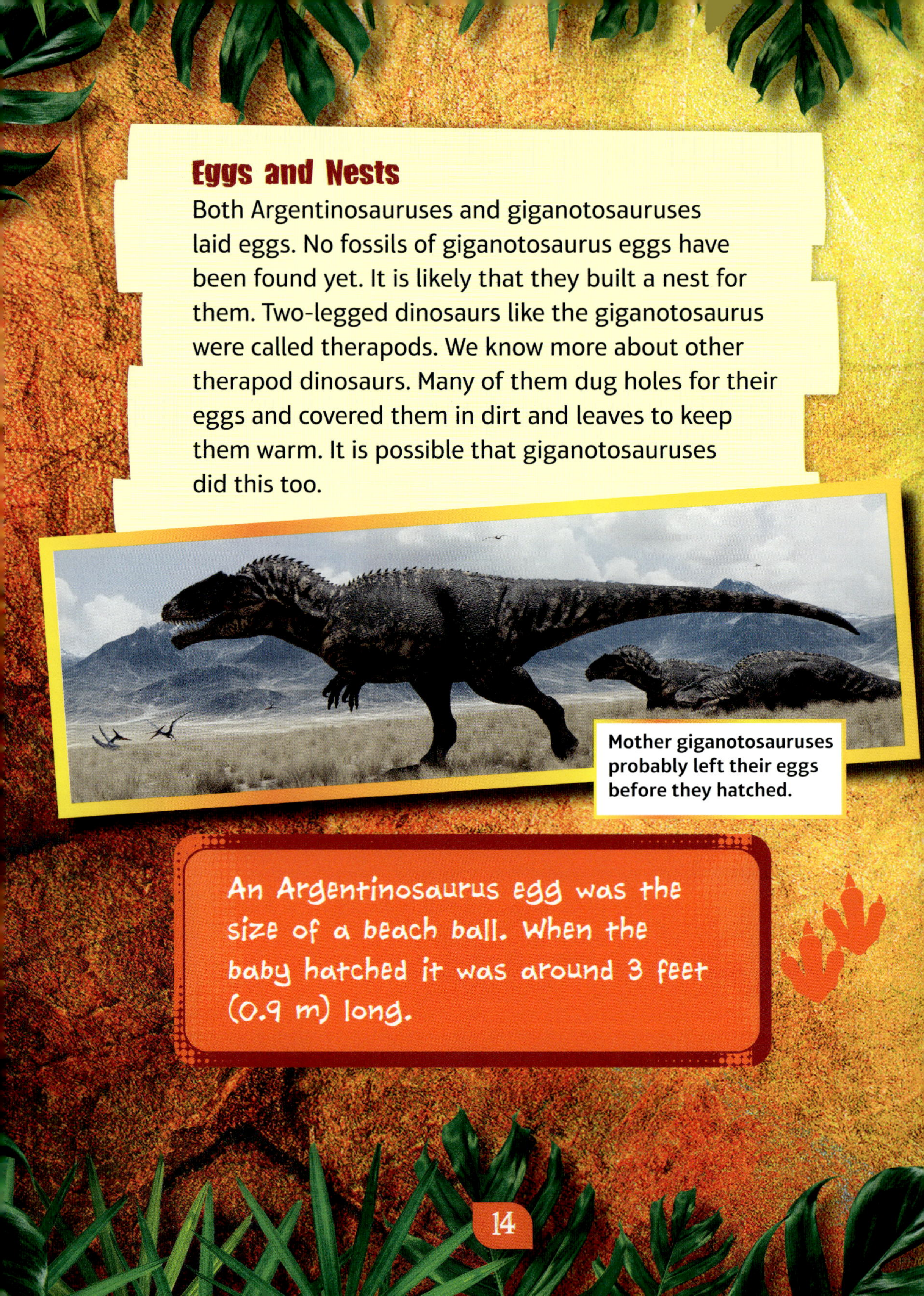

Mother giganotosauruses probably left their eggs before they hatched.

An Argentinosaurus egg was the size of a beach ball. When the baby hatched it was around 3 feet (0.9 m) long.

Only a few babies from each nest would survive to become adult Argentinosauruses.

Scientists know a lot more about Argentinosaurus nests. They gathered in large groups to build nests. Many kinds of sea birds do this today. Like sea birds, Argentinosauruses returned to the same place to breed, or make babies, each year. The giant dinosaurs dug a shallow pit and laid about thirty eggs inside.

Argentinosauruses could reach the leaves on trees that were too tall for other dinosaurs.

Growing Up

After hatching from its egg, a baby Argentinosaurus weighed about 11 pounds (5 kg). The tiny baby dinosaur would need a lot of protection! It took about fifteen years for the baby to grow to full size. An adult Argentinosaurus weighed at least fifteen thousand times more than the baby. That meant it needed to put on 35 pounds (16 kg) every day as it grew! The Argentinosaurus was one of the fastest-growing animals ever.

Argentinosauruses lived for around forty years. Giganotosauruses lived for less than thirty years. Few dinosaurs died of old age.

Giganotosauruses ate a lot of food, but they didn't eat very often.

It is likely that Argentinosauruses and giganotosauruses grew very fast when there was plenty of food. Argentinosauruses would have grown slower during droughts because the trees had fewer leaves. Giganotosauruses would have grown faster during the Argentinosaurus breeding season because they ate the baby dinosaurs.

Feeding Time

A giganotosaurus hunted for its meals when it could. At other times it stayed alive by being a scavenger. It looked for the bodies of large dinosaurs that had already died. It used its long, knife-like teeth to slice off chunks of meat to eat. The big dinosaur had to fight off other scavengers that wanted to eat this food.

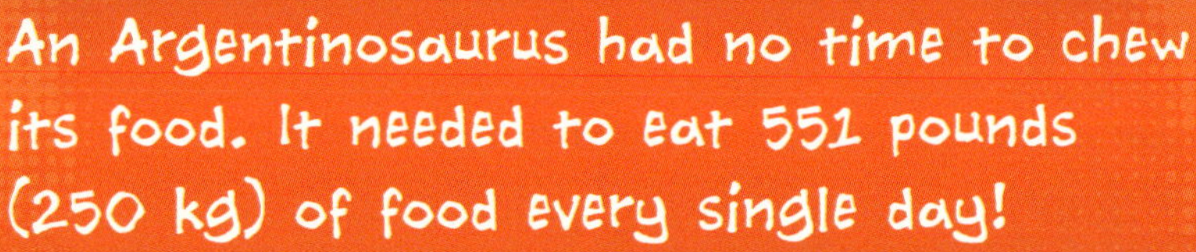

Huge stomach

Argentinosauruses spent most of the day eating. No teeth or skull fossils have been found for this dinosaur. Instead experts look at their relatives to find out more. Giant plant-eating dinosaurs were called titanosaurs. Other titanosaurs had very small teeth. They ate leaves and swallowed them whole. The leaves were then slowly digested inside the dinosaur's huge stomach.

Living Together

Dinosaur scientists think that both Argentinosauruses and giganotosauruses lived in groups. Argentinosauruses formed herds for safety, like deer do today. It was harder for a giganotosaurus to attack when there were a lot of Argentinosauruses around.

A herd of Argentinosauruses

Giganotosauruses probably lived in small groups called a pack. The pack worked together to hunt and kill animals that were much bigger than they were. Wolves live in packs. Like wolves, giganotosauruses would also hunt alone sometimes.

Giganotosauruses were not like most other dinosaurs. It is thought that they could warm their body and stay alert even when the weather was cold. Most dinosaurs could not do this.

Giganotosauruses had short arms with three claws on each hand. These may have helped them grab prey while the giganotosaurus was biting it.

An Argentinosaurus could wade in deep water to reach food.

Weapons

Argentinosauruses were plant-eating animals. They did not have weapons for fighting. As adults they were so huge, no hunting animals could attack them. Argentinosauruses also had armored skin. It was covered in thick lumps. These made it harder for predators to bite them.

Giganotosauruses were built to attack and kill other dinosaurs. They had dozens of long, triangular teeth. The shape of their skull tells us that giganotosauruses did not crush their prey with one powerful bite. It was more likely that they slashed and jabbed at prey over and over. This made many big cuts that would bleed a lot. Giganotosauruses would then follow their prey until it died from losing too much blood.

The giganotosaurus would travel long distances to find food.

CHOOSE YOUR WINNER

The giganotosaurus runs out of the forest. It charges at the herd of Argentinosauruses in the distance. They can see the predator now. Some bellow an alarm call. Most of the herd, including the babies, have crossed a river and are moving to safety. One of the adult Argentinosauruses is still on the same bank as the approaching attacker. It cannot run away. This Argentinosaurus will stand and fight.

The giganotosaurus does not attack right away. It circles the bigger animal looking to see how strong it is. The Argentinosaurus swings its tail at the giganotosaurus. It keeps its head up high, safely out of reach from its enemy's bites.

The giganotosaurus runs forward and jumps as high as it can on the side of the Argentinosaurus. It digs in its claws and bites into the skin. The knife-like teeth slice long cuts in the Argentinosaurus's skin. They start to bleed but are not a serious wound for such a big animal. The giganotosaurus falls to the ground. It must attack again.

After attacking the Argentinosaurus's neck, legs, and tail, the giganotosaurus is getting tired. It could hurt itself. It gives up and heads back to the forest. Today the Argentinosaurus is the winner. However, if the giganotosaurus comes back with its pack, then the fight could be very different. An attack at night would be bad. Or they could target the smaller members of the herd. Sometimes a giganotosaurus would be the winner in a fight with Argentinosauruses.

After a meal, a giganotosaurus's teeth would be full of bits of flesh. Some scientists think that a small dinosaur called an alvarezsaurus would carefully clean out the flesh and eat it. The giganotosaurus did not eat this helpful cleaner, and in return had healthy teeth.

The Argentinosaurus wins!

DINO DUEL

Giganotosaurus

- Powerful back legs
- Long tail
- Long claws
- Sharp teeth

Argentinosaurus

- Long neck
- Sturdy legs
- Armored skin
- Huge size

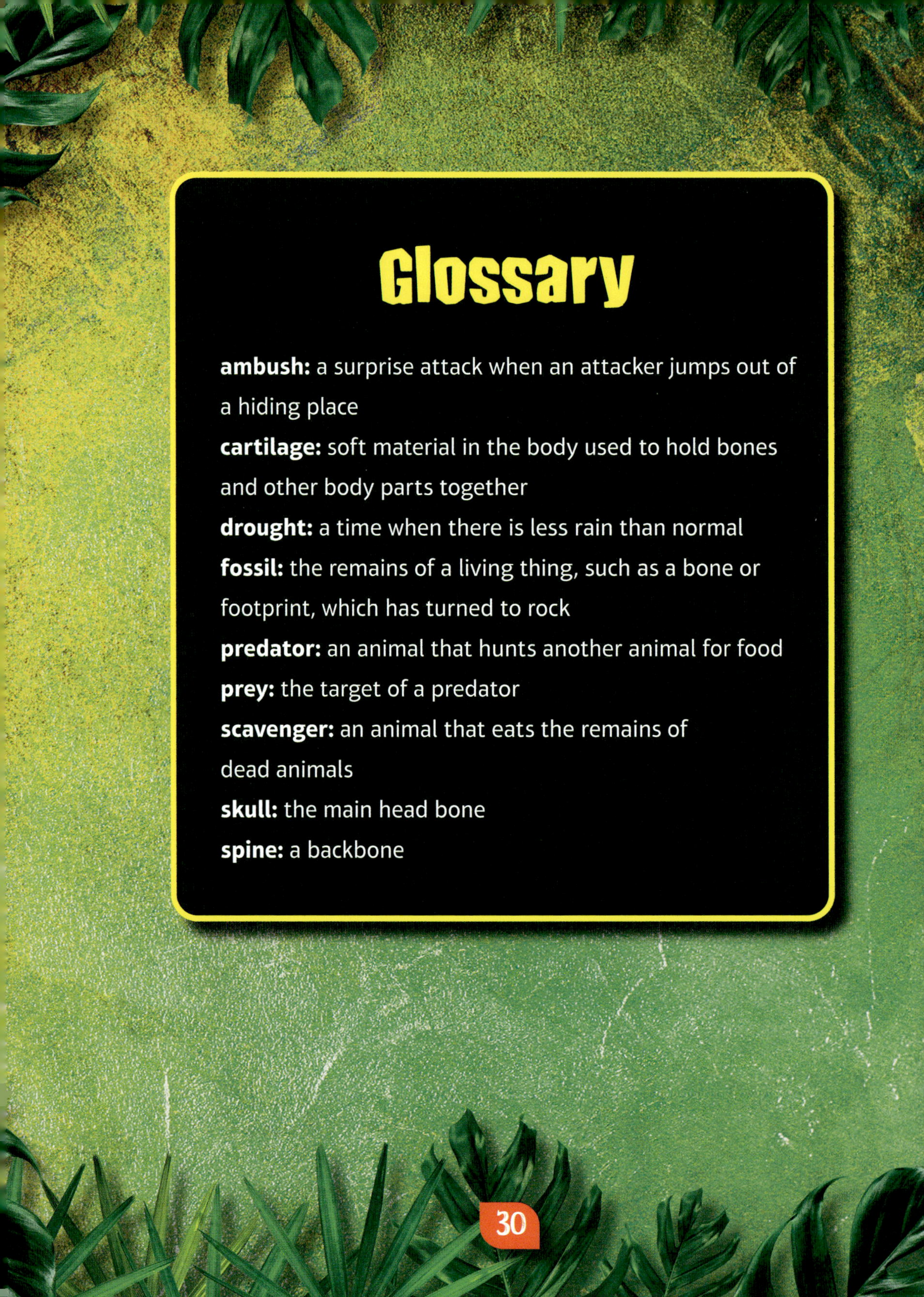

Glossary

ambush: a surprise attack when an attacker jumps out of a hiding place

cartilage: soft material in the body used to hold bones and other body parts together

drought: a time when there is less rain than normal

fossil: the remains of a living thing, such as a bone or footprint, which has turned to rock

predator: an animal that hunts another animal for food

prey: the target of a predator

scavenger: an animal that eats the remains of dead animals

skull: the main head bone

spine: a backbone

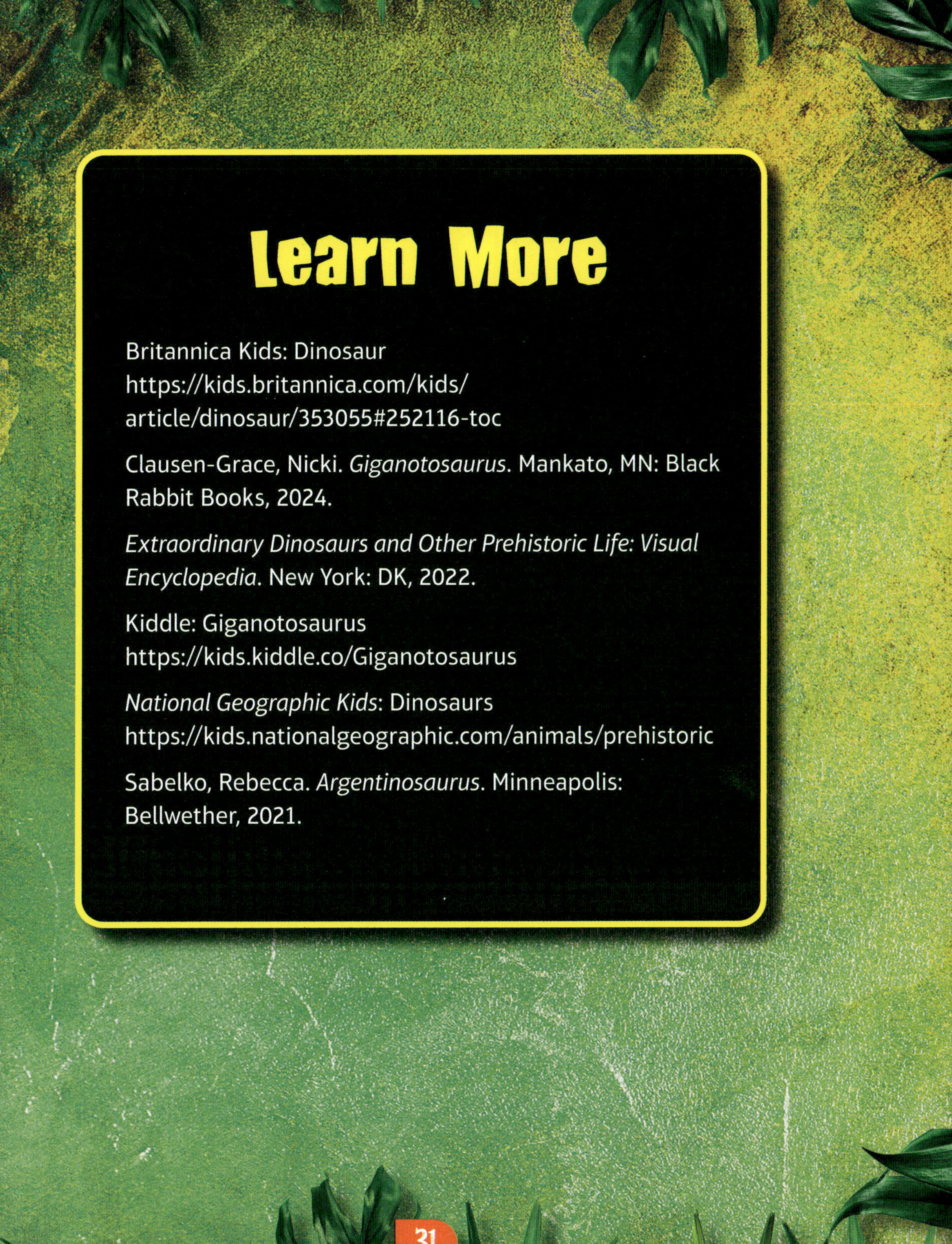

Learn More

Britannica Kids: Dinosaur
https://kids.britannica.com/kids/article/dinosaur/353055#252116-toc

Clausen-Grace, Nicki. *Giganotosaurus*. Mankato, MN: Black Rabbit Books, 2024.

Extraordinary Dinosaurs and Other Prehistoric Life: Visual Encyclopedia. New York: DK, 2022.

Kiddle: Giganotosaurus
https://kids.kiddle.co/Giganotosaurus

National Geographic Kids: Dinosaurs
https://kids.nationalgeographic.com/animals/prehistoric

Sabelko, Rebecca. *Argentinosaurus*. Minneapolis: Bellwether, 2021.

Index

Photo Acknowledgments

Image credits: Liidia/Shitterstock, p. 1; Daniel Eskridge/Dreamstime.com, p. 4; Mr1805/Dreamstime.com, pp. 5, 19–20, 24–25; Michael Rosskothen/Shutterstock, pp. 6, 18; Kamomeen/Shutterstock, p. 7a; Herschel Hoffmeyer/Shutterstock, pp. 7b, 10–12, 14, 23; Jonathon Chen/Wikimedia Commons p. 8; Etemenanki3/Wikimedia Commons, p. 9; Warpaint/Shutterstock, pp. 13, 27; Elenarts/Shutterstock, pp. 15–16; ishibashi seiichi/Shutterstock, p. 17; Corey A Ford/Dreamstime.com, p. 21; Elena Duvernay/Dreamstime.com, p. 22; Mark Turner/Dreamstime.com, p. 28; Inna Markova/Dreamstime.com, p. 29. Design elements: Kompaniets Taras/Shutterstock; Chaiyapong/Shutterstock; Liidia/Shutterstock.

Cover: Dmitrii Sakharov/Shutterstock (top); Warpaint/Shutterstock (top), (bottom); Maria_Gb/Shutterstock (bottom).